The Skeletons Are Out

The Skeletons Are Out

Kenya Richardson

To order additional copies of this book, contact:
Xlibris Corporation
1-888-795-4274
www.Xlibris.com
Orders@Xlibris.com
58473

Dedication

I would like to dedicate this book to all young ladies who have been through similar events that I have been through. It was hard experiencing things and not being able to trust anyone to talk to about them. There are a lot of eight-year-olds and ten-year-olds who have experienced molestation and rape and can't trust anyone to tell. It has taken me twenty-five years to release the frustration, guilt, and emotional pain. If you have experienced similar events, try to find it in your heart to forgive those who have caused you pain so you can move forward in life and achieve what God has for you. I thank God for covering me all these years, and I know that because of what happened to me at an early age, he has protected me and forgiven me for all the wrong that I've done. I know now that it was not my fault, and I wish I had the courage then to tell someone what I was going through, and my life probably wouldn't have gone the way it went. If you are a teenager and have been molested or raped by anyone, please tell someone. It is not healthy for you to carry the guilt or burden of such a tragedy. God can deliver you, and he will heal you, if you let him. Don't do like what I have done and wait twenty-five years to release it. If you do, your life will be full of heartaches, pain, and disappointments. You will be in a constant battle with your emotions, and it will lead you to a number of unhealthy relationships.

Dear Mommy and Daddy

Dear Mommy,

To all those who are mothers and to those who someday will be, please watch over your daughters. Don't be too consumed with your everyday living and forget your precious jewels. God holds you accountable for all your children go through. Boys are a little different – they can stand their ground, but girls need that extra attention and the extra nourishing.

Watch what you do around your daughters, and don't do around them anything that they can't do around you. Establish a lasting relationship with your daughters, and make them comfortable enough to talk to you about anything.

Teach your daughters how to become young ladies, how to respect themselves and their bodies. If we don't teach our children, the streets will, and nobody knows this better than me.

Dear Daddy,

To all who are fathers or one day will be, take pride in being a father. Anyone can be a daddy, but it takes a real man to be a father. So many young people in America aren't fortunate enough to have a responsible father. Men are deadbeat dads, leaving the responsibility to the mother. If you don't want to be a father, don't have sex unprotected. A father's love means so much to children, especially to young girls.

Take the time to evaluate your relationship with your daughter. Do you take her to the park? Do you take her to the movies? Do you take her shopping? Do you spend any quality time with her? If not, designate a day to spend with her, at least once a month. It's time to heal our women, the mother, and the daughter, and the grandmother.

If every father in the world would do their part in raising children, there wouldn't be so many diseases, teen pregnancies, black-on-black crimes, and abortions. Spend time with your daughters; give them the love they deserve, and they will not look for it in the streets.

Disney World 1983

I WAS AN eight-year-old who attracted a sixteen-year-old female and, two years later, a fifteen-year-old female and a sixty-year-old man. I don't know what motivated these individuals to do what they did to me, but it stripped me of my innocence. It made me shy away from everyone, creating a sense of loneliness and depression at an early age.

Every weekend, I would go over my friend's house and stay until Sunday. We went to church together, so I wanted to go every weekend to get away from all my brothers. Until after our trip to Disney World. My friend had an older sister, and I had to sleep in the bed with her on our trip. One night, their mom and dad went out to eat. My friend was asleep in her parents' bed, so her big sister crawled in the bed with me. She pulled my panties down and began to put her fingers inside me. She made my vagina wet; only thing was, I didn't know what I was supposed to be feeling, but she did. She went down and began to put her mouth on my vagina. She stuck her tongue inside it, and then she put her hands over my mouth as she lay on top of me. She moved her body up and down until her body started trembling, and she got up.

After we got back, I didn't want to go over to their house as much. Instead of telling my friend what her sister had done to me, I began to show her. I asked her if she wanted to play doctor. I was the doctor, and I wanted to look at her private parts. That was my way of telling someone because I couldn't tell a soul. I was too embarrassed, and I didn't want to have to stop going over my friend's house. But I felt that her sister would do it again, and she did. One night, I spent the night over there, and I slept in the bed with her sister. She did it again. And this time, she made my body tremble all over. I was eight years old, and I had my first encounter of an orgasm.

I went to third grade at Fair Park Elementary. Mrs. Gill was the principal, and Mrs. Marilyn Turner was my third-grade teacher. I couldn't get in much trouble because Mrs. Gill knew my aunt Lilly. I had a fight with Katrina Robinson; we lived at 1024 S. Washington, and Katrina lived three houses up from me. We were always competing for something. She got a paddle, and Mrs. Gill told me not to get into any more trouble, or she would call my aunt.

My two oldest brothers went to Central High, and the oldest was the president of the student body. All my brothers were athletes, and they all were honor roll students. My oldest brother had a so-called friend who would come over our house and put me on his lap. Lee would stick his fingers in my vagina and wiggle his fingers around in it. He had long fingernails, and it would scratch me every time he did it. I wanted to tell someone, but I thought I would get in trouble. Instead of telling, I began wanting this feeling.

I was going to the fourth grade at Pulaski Heights Intermediate. My brother was in the sixth grade, and Keemo was in the eighth grade at Pulaski Heights Junior High, and they both had a lot of friends. I had a lot of friends also, and I stayed on the principal's list. I wanted to follow my big brother's footsteps. My fourth-grade year was great. I made a lot of new friends, and I was looking forward to being at the school without my big brother.

I stopped going over my friend's house so much and started hanging out at my cousin's house. She was older than me and had a lot of older friends; I also had friends who lived across the street from her. My cousin had a boyfriend, and we used to listen to New Edition, Whitney Houston, and the Gap band while I played with her Barbie dolls. I didn't own any, so every time I went over there, that's all I wanted to do until her father put me in a situation like my friend's sister had.

One day, everybody left my cousin's house. They went to get something to eat, and I was left alone with her father. He received a

Purple Heart from the military; he had stepped on a land mine when he was in Vietnam. It affected his speech, and it also affected his manhood. I was walking to the bathroom when he grabbed me by the arm. He turned me around so my back would be to him. He put his hand down my pants and began to rub my vagina. He was grinding my booty as his fingers were going in and out my vagina. He told me it was his vagina, and I couldn't give it to anybody but him. He let me go, and I went to the bathroom and washed up.

Later that night, he told me to come lay on the bed with him. I did because I was only ten and didn't know any better, and I didn't want to get in trouble. When I got on his bed, he pulled my gown up and began to caress my vagina with his hand. This time, he made me feel like my friend's sister had made me feel. When he was done, he told me to go get back in the bed with his daughter. I was so nervous because I didn't know whether to tell her or to keep it to myself. So I decided to keep it to myself. As the night went on, my cousin reached over and put her hands down my panties. I started thinking, is this what people are supposed to do to me? She played with my vagina, sticking her fingers in and out of me. She made me have the same feelings that her dad and my friend's sister had made me feel. I was ten years old, and I had two orgasms in one day.

The next day, I went home, and I couldn't tell a soul about what had happened to me. I started to shy away from my family, and I began wanting this feeling all the time. I began to notice boys a lot more, and I began to get rebellious toward my mom. I wanted to tell her about what I had experienced, but I couldn't. I felt like this may have been my fault, and what would people say about me? But in the end, I was still talked about.

I played softball for One Trip Beauty Supply over the summer. Smoky and Boobee were our coaches. Boobee's little sister, Crystal, and I were friends, and that's how I got on the team. I was a cheerleader when I was six and seven for my brothers' football team, but I had never played any organized sports. I enjoyed it, and I really enjoyed going over Crystal's house after the games.

Crystal's dad owned the club, Quarter Note, and they had lip syncs every Sunday night. Boobee took me to the club, and I lip-synced Whitney Houston's "You Give Good Love." I almost won; I just didn't have on the right clothes. I enjoyed it, and I got a lot of compliments. That showed me, at a young age, that I was definitely an entertainer.

The summer was almost over, and I was going to fifth grade. I made straight As, and I was very active in school. After all I went through over the summer, I began to distance myself from my family. I didn't want anyone to know what I had been through, so I never told a soul. My family life looked perfect on the outside, but up close and personal, it was a mess. My father had been heavily addicted to drugs, and he was physically abusive to my mother. I remember waking up one morning to them fighting; I cried as I begged him to stop hitting her. He looked at me, and he left the house.

Ten years old and already pleasing men and young women, I didn't know what was in store for me for the rest of my life. I remained on the honor roll and active in school. I was gifted and talented; Mrs. Rouse was the wife of my friend's father, so she made sure I stayed focused. I started hanging out with girls who were already sexually active. We skipped school and walked to University Mall. We didn't get caught, and I couldn't believe skipping school could be so fun. When we got back over my friend's house, the boys wanted us to have sex with them, but I told them I had to go home, and I left. She must have agreed, and she ended up pregnant.

As an eleven-year-old sixth grader at Pulaski Heights Elementary, I was the student body president, and I was friends with everyone at the school. I had formed my own group, the LaTy Ks – Kim B., Kesha, Kim G., Terry, and me. We took up dues, $1 a month, to buy candy and Kool-Aid that we mixed with sugar in a ziplock bag to eat, and we would spend the night at each other's house.

Kim B. and I had been friends since kindergarten. We walked to school together, and I adored her mom and dad. She had older brothers and sisters, a nephew, and two nieces. We stayed on Thirteenth and she stayed on Fourteenth and Martin. Her brother Steve and my brother Kaelon were friends. Kesha was my road dog. Her brother and my brother Keemo were best friends. She had two big brothers and a lot of cousins. Kim G. was new to Pulaski Heights; she had a white mother and a black father, and she lived up the street from the school. She had an older brother who went to the junior high and was friends with my brother Keemo. Terry was from the neighborhood, and she had been at Pulaski Heights all three years with us. She lived off Eleventh Street, around the corner from me. We had other people who wanted to be in our group, but I wouldn't let anyone else in. I also had one other friend, LaShonda, and even though she wasn't in our group, we were still friends. She lived off Fourteenth and Abigail, and she had an older brother, who was my brother Kevin's age.

School was so fun, especially at lunch; I would go to the teachers' lounge and take their trays back to the cafeteria. We shared cafeterias with the junior high school, and when they went to lunch, we were back in class. I had the biggest crush on Darryl M. He was a star basketball player. I knew exactly what time they would be in the cafeteria, so I always took the teachers' lunch trays back. I always figured out a way to get on the junior high side. I had a brother who attended there, so I tried not to let him see me being so mischievous. I remember saying we had to learn and practice an African dance and we were allowed to go over to the auditorium on the junior high side to learn a dance; I made one up and performed it in class.

I was a straight-A student who loved to write letters, and one day, I had a letter intercepted by a girl's mom. She went to Southwest Junior High, and I had a crush on Yancy; he was so fine to me. I gave Cece the letter, and it must have dropped out of her backpack. My mom brought me the letter, and I couldn't say a word. She didn't fuss; all she said was, "Respectable young ladies don't write letters asking a boy to have sex." I was embarrassed for a day but soon got over it.

Out of all my classes, I loved Mrs. Rouse's math class and music class. I was in the gifted and talented class; we were on the upper level of the school. Pulaski Heights Intermediate and Pulaski Heights Junior High were connected by the auditorium and the cafeteria. The school's race ratio was even.

As my sixth-grade year came to an end, we had a substitute teacher in social studies, and I felt like being the class clown, so I mooned the class. I would not have gotten caught if Nicholas and Latavius hadn't told on me. They impeached me from being the president, and I didn't get to go on the end-of-the-year field trip to Burns Park. That hurt my feelings, but it taught me a valuable lesson: stop showing my ass.

The summer of 1986 I went to the Mid-South drug rehab conference in Fayetteville, Arkansas, with my mom, dad, little sisters, and brother. It was my debut; I got a chance to perform with my father in front of hundreds of people. We sang "Suddenly, Seymour." It was a moment I could never forget. I loved my father, but he didn't know how to love me back.

Although my father abused drugs, my mother, and his body, he was still a caring man. He grew up without a mother. She burned up in a neighbor's house when he was three, and his father was killed by a policeman when he was a young boy. My aunt Vivian and my great-grandmother raised him, his brother, and his sister.

I longed to have a relationship with my father, but everything else occupied his time. He was a man that had much respect in Little Rock, Arkansas. He worked for the circuit court. He had a band called Recovery. He went through the original Gyst House program, and he played the organ at a church. I wanted to be just like my dad, and in a sense, I did.

Church

A T FAITH TEMPLE Baptist Church, Rev. L. A. Lindsey was the pastor. I loved my church. My father played the piano, and my mother sang in the choir. My brothers were either ushers or choir members. I chose to sing in the choir and be mischievous with my friend. She was already having sex, but I didn't know if her sister had ever done to her what she had done to me. She told me about having sex in the car with a local pastor, and it made me look at ministers a lot different. But all I knew was Faith Temple. We didn't go to any other churches.

We took a trip to the skating rink one night over the summer. Jam and I decided to be fast and rode with some of the guys from the church. They asked if they could run a train on us, and she said okay, so I said okay; I didn't know what a train was. She went first. Three of the guys all got in the back of the station wagon with her, and all I remember was the car having a bad odor. They asked me if I wanted to go next. Two of the boys were excited, but the third one said I was too young, and he didn't want to be a part of that; I guess he was the only true "chosen" one. Well, the preacher's son went first, but his thing would not go in. I was still a virgin even though I had been molested a year before. After he couldn't get in, the deacon's son said to let him try. He didn't get in either, but he rubbed his penis up against me so hard, he came. I thought I was all that; little did I know I had been set up for a world of fornication.

I became a fiend for sex. I thought that was the only way to get a guy's attention, to tell him I wasn't a virgin. After the night with the guys in the car, nobody ever said a word about it, and we continued going to the church until the pastor wouldn't let my mother keep her day care at the church.

I was beginning my seventh grade year at the junior high, and I was ready. I had four boyfriends; I didn't have sex with them, and I just talked to them on the phone and wrote them letters. My friend went to Southwest Junior High, and I had a boyfriend at her school, and she had one at mine. I loved writing notes and meeting new people. The ninth-grade boys were scared to talk to me because my brother went there, and my cousin was the coach.

I managed to get a ninth-grade boyfriend at my school named Bang. He was a star player on the basketball team at the school; he just had a lot of girlfriends. When I finally decided to let him be my boyfriend, he propositioned me. He had friends that I was cool with, Derrick and Tim, and then he had a few guys on the basketball team he was cool with.

After Keemo died, my mom put a perm in my hair, and I used to get my hair done at World of Curls by Mrs. Eubanks. And Lamont's mom, Kay, would perm it sometimes. I would go over to their apartment in Westbridge, building X, on Fridays, and she would drop me off at home when she got done. Lamont had a friend named Gavin, whom I was in love with. He was in high school, though, so I thought he would never give me the time of day, not a twelve-year-old. I flirted with Gavin every time I went over Lamont's house. I think, after a while, he began to like me, too. He never disrespected me nor did he ever try to sleep with me. Bang, on the other hand, that's all he talked about. I knew he was having sex because of the girls he was going with. I was just a seventh grader, so I had to do the things the ninth-grade girls were doing in order to keep my ninth-grade boyfriend.

I decided to have sex with Bang. We were over Lamont's house, and Bang, Lamont, and two of the other basketball players were there. Kay left to run an errand, and all the boys convinced me that it wouldn't be that bad. They made sure Bang had a condom and told us to go in the bathroom, in case Kay came home. We lay on the floor and had sex. It was not all that, I thought to myself. It didn't feel anything like my previous experiences. But I finally had it out of the way. My virginity was gone.

After me and Bang had sex, he wasn't interested in me anymore. No one knew but the boys who were over there that night, or so I thought. Bang told all his friends. Derrick wrote me a letter, acting like he was Bang, to let me know he had been talking. I had no one to blame but me; I should have known he was the typical boy, bragging about what he accomplished.

I liked Bang because he grew up in a rough situation. His sister Lena and I were cool in the sixth grade, and his grandmother raised them. Lena had a large portion of her body scalded as a child Her face down had been burned, but she was still allowed to attend school. She was so strong, and I admired her ambition. Bang loved his sister, and he gave her whatever she wanted. After we broke up, another basketball player wanted to talk to me, guess he had heard about me and Bang.

A girl that went to my church had a brother named Chris; they went to Pulaski Heights, and they lived across the street from the school. Chris used to always tell me he wanted to give me something. One day, I went over their house after school, and her brother was there. She told me to go in his room. When I got in there, he was naked. He told me he wanted to eat me. I let him eat me, and then he asked me if he could play with my vagina. I let him, and after he got through, he told me to go wash up and not to tell anybody, and I didn't. We did a duet at the school's talent show, and we had the whole school screaming for us.

I was glad that I was almost in the eighth grade. I wanted to go to Central High; the junior high boys were getting boring to me, in addition, the ninth graders were leaving for high school. I joined Y-Teens; it was a predominantly white group, but I was friends with everybody. Catherine Usery became one of my good friends; she happened to be white. I spent the night over her house one Friday night. She lived in the Heights, by St. John's School. We sneaked out the house at two in the morning to meet some of the other girls from school. They all brought a drink. We were seventh graders, and I didn't know anything about drinking, and after that night, I didn't want to know anything else about it. We all met up at the water tower. It was around the corner from Catherine's house. We sat there, talking and drinking, and we decided to walk through St. John's. I had to pee really badly, and we couldn't go to any of their houses because we were not supposed to be out. I had on a pair of yellow Levi's, and I pissed all over myself. When we got in, Catherine put my pants in the washer. I was really looking forward to the rest of my junior high years.

The cheerleaders went to camp in Arkadelphia, and it was great. I learned a lot that summer, and I became the best front herkie jumper in my class. I loved to cheer the team on, and I made sure everybody heard me. I was the captain of the cheerleaders, I played volleyball and basketball, and I ran track.

Junior High School

MY MOM WAS always working and seeing about the five of us, along with all her grown children. My dad was out being a ho. He had five children on my mother. I don't know why she stayed with him so long. I guess so we can have a male figure in our lives. The male figure I looked up to had died. Keemo was my positive example, and after he died, I ended up getting nothing but negative results.

My thirteenth birthday was next month, and I wanted to plan another big party like the year before. I was a seventh-grade honor roll student at Pulaski Heights Junior High. I was on the drill team, I played volleyball and basketball, I ran track, and I played the violin. I was very popular among my friends. I was the first daughter out of five boys, and the sixth child out of nine. Light skin, long hair, and bowed legs –I was your typical around-the-way girl. I hung around mostly with ninth graders, Natasha Saine and Rosetta Jackson, but I still had my best friends since kindergarten. My cousin was the coach at the school, and he was also the gym teacher. I decided to have my birthday party in the school gym because it was big and there would be plenty of space. I had a friend named Tory Smith, who shared my birthday with me, and I called him to see if he wanted to have a party with me. He thought it would be cool, so I planned it all out. I invited the entire school, plus my family. I hired a DJ and decided to order pizza and cake. Tory was a student at Dunbar Junior High School, and he lived in the South End projects. Tory and I became friends at the South End community center, and I also had a crush on his cousin, Li'l Richard. March 29, 1988, was the day I had been waiting on. I was finally thirteen, and it hit me – my brother didn't make it to see me turn thirteen.

It was a chilly Tuesday night, December 15, 1987, me and my brother Kaelon rode the bus home after our basketball game. I still had on my basketball uniform, and I couldn't wait to tell Keemo that I had gotten in the varsity game. As we got to the corner of Thirteenth and Johnson, I recognized my godfather Neal's van. I told Kaelon it looked like Neal was at the house. He got off the bus first, and I eagerly got off behind him. I couldn't wait to tell Keemo how I did at the game. Neal's daughter, Teekie, stopped me, and she said Keemo collapsed on the basketball court at practice; and just as she was telling me, Kaelon stormed out the door. Then she said, "He didn't make it." I burst into tears.

He was at UAMS Hospital, and when we walked up to the emergency room, I saw all his classmates from Central High crying uncontrollably. We went through the sliding doors. I remember my mother's face, and it looked as if she had lost her heart. I couldn't cry because I felt someone had to be strong; they asked us if we wanted to go back and see him one last time. I nodded my head yes. I couldn't believe my brother was dead. I walked into the cold white room, still dressed in my uniform, and gazed at my brother lying on the bed; he looked like he was asleep. His eyes looked like they had Vaseline on them, and he had cream in his nostrils. I kissed his forehead and told him I loved him and walked out the room.

It seemed like it took forever to have his funeral. My aunt from California came. My oldest brother lived in California, and he came home. My sister from Detroit came. Everybody in Little Rock, Arkansas, was at my brother's funeral. I held up good until both Kims walked around to view his body. He was in love with them; he walked Kim Mays on the football homecoming court, and Kim Franklin was his girlfriend. As soon as I looked at them, tears began to roll down my face. When it was time for the family to view, I went up first; I kissed my brother on his forehead again and told him I loved him. My mom didn't want to let go. She screamed, "Why?" I couldn't answer her, but I knew it was God's will. Freeman and Son's Funeral Home handled the arrangements. As they escorted the family out, I walked by myself, and it seemed as if everybody had someone to hold them up except for me. When I got in the limousine, I closed my eyes and prayed. When I woke up, we were at the cemetery, Haven of Rest, on Twelfth Street. It was raining as they escorted us out the limo to the grave site.

The next weekend, I spent the night over Kesha's house; her brother and Keemo were best friends. I started my menstruation cycle, and I didn't know how to tell my mom, so I wrote her a note. I knew she was still grieving from the loss of my brother, but I was having some real-life issues, and it seemed as if no one cared.

Junior High

I THOUGHT I was grown at the age of thirteen. I had no direction after Keemo died, and I turned to the streets for guidance, and this was where it got me.

February 1989, Tory got killed. Everybody started calling me, giving me their versions of what happened. They said he was playing Russian roulette. They said one of the boys at the table did it. Man, I was crushed; we planned on having another party together the next month. I really felt sorry for his cousin, Li'l Richard. He had gotten locked up, and Tory and I were there the day he got arrested.

Tory, Richard, and I were at the South End community center, and Richard and I were in the game room, playing tic-tac-toe. Tory ran through the side door, yelling, "Richard, the police are everywhere. Man, you better get out of here." Richard took off out the back door, and I sat there, like, what the hell was going on? I was only thirteen. I didn't have a clue. I wanted to be hard and rebel against what everybody said about him, but it was true. Richard was wanted by the police. He ran all the way through the South End projects and made it to the freeway, and he said he heard the police lady say, "Get down, or I'll shoot." He said he threw his hands up and got down, and he was gone for a long time.

He lived in Highland Court Projects, and his life was the streets. I guess that's why I liked Richard so much. He didn't fear anything. I remember being involved in my first drive-by shooting. Richard,

THE SKELETONS ARE OUT

Tory, and I were walking down Fourteenth and Peyton. A car slowed down, and I heard a guy say, "There goes Richard." Next thing I knew, gunshots started ringing out the car. Richard told me to get down, and after the car had passed us, we got up, and he told me I had to go back home. It tripped me out, but I went back home.

When Richard left, I started hanging out at the South End community center. My brother worked there, and when I played softball for One Trip Beauty Supply, we practiced there.

I kept in touch with Li'l Richard. We wrote, but I started looking at the high school boys. I had a senior who was well known at the school. He had high-executive uncles in the streets. He called me Tracy, and I called him Bryan; that's so no one would find out about us. He was so sweet, and I loved leaving zero hour to be with him in the mornings. I would get out of class, and we would go over his cousin Herb's house and be together until it was time for me to be at Pulaski Heights.

Bryan piqued a lot of older guys' curiosity when he couldn't keep it a secret anymore. They began to speak to me at school as I was leaving and gave me their numbers. I had a boyfriend at Pulaski Heights, but we only dated at school. Looking on the outside, you would think I had it all together, but I became distant. And even though I was outgoing at school, I hated my life at home.

I met Ricky at the South End community center. He was eighteen, and, boy, did I like him. He was just a dog, had four girlfriends, and I was just a young pup, sniffing around where I didn't have no business. But, boy, did I give him a run for his money. Rick was the local weed boy. He had it and always had it. He kept a lot from me, but I knew deep in his heart he cared for me. Rick and I went to Tory's funeral together. He helped me get over Tory's death. He hid my best friend when she ran away from home. He taught me the rough side of life, and he taught me how to be the dog I became. He was eighteen, had his own place, and loved his family. He had Lori, Tamika, me, and whoever else he went with at the time. I was the youngest of them all.

I never had beef with Lori, Tamika, or any of Rick's girls, but gossip and rumors started a fight at Hall and Central's basketball game, and one of Tamika's friends got stabbed several times. Rick didn't allow me to fight. He threw me in the car and told Joe to take me from out there. I knew then that I had created some monsters claiming I was in a gang. We were the Lady Pimpin' Bloods – me, Tasha, April L., Peaches, M. Johns, and several others that had their own clique. The fight was supposed to be between me and Tamika over Rick, but I had some young wild and crazy girls with me because that's what I had become. We thought we were the hardest things walking around Little Rock, Arkansas.

Rick had so many girlfriends; I decided I would get me two or three more boyfriends. Little did I know, he knew them all. I didn't care; he was a dog, so I was going to be one too.

My fourteenth birthday was coming up so I decided, since Tory wasn't there, I was going to do something small with my closest friends. Shonda, Bill, Cedric, Keenan, M. Johns, AG, Tamika, and I had pizza and cake at my house on Thirteenth Street. I was fourteen and ready for the world.

I went to the eighth-grade prom; I wore a purple dress, the same dress I wore to the ball at church. Mrs. Sutton and Mr. Freeman chaperoned the prom. My eighth-grade year was coming to a close, and as I began to get older, I began to attract older men.

My oldest brother was the road manager for the group Club Nouveau. We went to Kentucky for a concert, and I got onstage to do the "Pump It Up"; it was a dance they sung about. He dated Val, the lead singer in the group. They traveled the world, and I loved all the shoes and coats he had us made overseas.

We went to cheerleading camp in Arkadelphia again. This time it was more fun. Shantese and Kendra and I had our cheerleading team off the chain. We won all the categories at camp, and we even had fun in the dorms. Shantese and I were roommates, and we stayed up singing New Edition all night long. We had so much fun.

As my ninth grade started, we had a good volleyball and basketball team. I was the president of the school, and we had a ball. Our school ranked highest academically, and our boys had a good football and basketball team. We had dances once a month in the gym, and we always had a good time. I was still going to Central High for zero-hour orchestra class.

My school boyfriend was Wes Flanigan. I liked Wes, but I had gotten too used to the thugs. We would sit on the bus together after the games, and we would write each other letters. I represented our school at a lot of functions – FBLA, Beta Club, Junior Honor Society – and in sports. A perfect picture from the outside, but a living hell on the inside.

The Funeral Home

IT SEEMED LIKE every day, someone was dying, and I knew them. September 1989, my cousin Gary got killed. I was at Fairfield Bay with my parents. My father's band was playing at the resort for a Mid-South drug and rehab conference. My mother walked in my room and told me Gary had gotten killed. I immediately jumped up. I replayed my mother's words, and immediately, tears began to roll down my face. All I could think about was what could have happened. I had just started getting close to Gary. Me, him, Nikki, and Fellow would all hang out together in Woodson and just have fun. We walked through the entire town, got chased by dogs, and threw rocks, and we just had fun. We got back to Little Rock, and I found out what happened. This girl was at the dollar movies in Southwest off Geyer Springs and I-30, and Gary, Fellow, and some more of their friends tried to holler at this girl. Her boyfriend got mad, followed my cousin and four of his friends, who were riding on the back of an open bed truck, and the boy opened fire on them. Gary was the only one that got shot. Man, I was devastated. Fellow took it hard too; he and Gary were best friends. They had been friends since they were little boys. Fifteen and dead. I really started acting out of character. I was a freshman at Pulaski Heights Junior High, captain of the cheerleading team and basketball team, president of the student council, and member of the Central High orchestra.

My parents had divorced, so my household was very rocky. I know I created some of those rocky mountains because I didn't want to hear what nobody had to say. I remember trying to get Sylvia to drop me off over Rick's house, and my brother Kaelon and I had a big fight. We broke out my mom's window, and I hit him with the telephone. I couldn't see that he was only trying to protect me. I didn't want any direction because I felt like nobody cared anyway. I had a brother who had just got home from prison, one traveling around the world with Club Nouveau, one trying to find his purpose, one dead, one brother wanting to be me, my little brother and sisters' father. He couldn't do it all, and I didn't want anyone to feel like they were taking care of me. I could take care of myself.

Rick used to pay to get my hair done by Marilyn every Friday. She worked at LeHair Gallery with Paula Sims; I used to admire them both because they were getting paid. The shop was on Twelfth Street, off Fair Park. Marilyn had my hair down my back, and it stayed healthy.

Stacey and her cousin Nef used to keep their hair fly by Marilyn; everybody that was connected to Marilyn used to keep their hair fly. I used to spend the night over Stacey's grandmother's house around the corner from Central. I used to walk over to Rick's house from there. Stacey and I did everything together, and she never had anything bad to say about what all I did. She knew all my boyfriends because they used to come over her grandmother's house to see me. She had an uncle who wanted to sleep with me, and one day, he told me to come in the back room. He lifted up my skirt and put his penis in. He covered my mouth with his hands so I wouldn't express my feelings. He came in one minute. I was shocked he did it right there, but I knew he liked me. He had for a while; he just never had the opportunity to sex me until then. He was about eleven years older than me, and he had plenty of money. All of Stacey's family did. Her uncles were big-time dealers back in the day, and they made sure that their family was taken care of.

Rick and I did everything together, but I knew in the back of my mind that he had several other girlfriends, so I let him take me out, buy me things, and sex me whenever and wherever.

My ninth-grade year was going good. I was juggling school, and I also had to juggle my boyfriends. Rick was my main squeeze, but I flirted with several other guys. Manny liked me, but I would never talk to him because he went with my friend AG. He had been trying to talk to me ever since we were in the seventh grade. He left in the eighth grade, went to juvenile. He had a gun on the school bus and pulled it out, saying, "Nobody move, nobody gets hurt." The bus hit a pothole, and the gun went off, shooting a girl in the arm. When I saw that on the news, I called AG and asked her if she saw the news. She said yeah, but she didn't go with him anymore. I asked her if I could talk to him. She said she didn't care. Her sister used to talk to him. That didn't surprise me after what her sister did to me. He wrote me letters while he was in juvenile, telling me he wanted us to hook up; I told him I would see.

Basketball season was getting ready to start. I loved basketball, and ever since Keemo had died, all I wanted to do was play ball because that was his favorite sport. M. Johns, Tamika, Javonne, Shantese, and I were the starting five. We made it to the playoffs – February 1990, Pulaski Heights against Horace Mann. The third quarter, we were leading. I was dribbling the ball down the court, and my knee went out. I fell to the floor but jumped back up. I wanted to win so bad. We would have been city champs. Coach Landrith came on the court and picked me up. I sat on the bench, and Coach Williams got me an ice pack. I wanted to go back in the game for the fourth quarter, but when I ran up the court, I fell again. This time Coach Williams told me I had torn my ACL, and that I had to go to the hospital. My coach took me to the hospital because nobody ever came to my games. It was true: I had torn my ACL. I was devastated. The only thing I cared about since Keemo died was taken away from me. The doctor told me I would have to have surgery, and I could rehab my knee and play next year. I didn't want to wait until next year. I walked on crutches for the next two weeks until my surgery was scheduled. It was hard getting around at Central for my zero-hour orchestra class, so I started skipping school with Bryan. I liked him, but he knew my brothers wouldn't approve, so we saw each other when no one knew it.

It was then I let the devil take me down memory lane. I couldn't play ball, so all I did was sit on my front porch at 3108 W. Thirteenth, Little Rock, Arkansas – a house located in between the Crips and the Bloods. A large portion of my friends were Bloods, but I also associated with a lot of Crips. Crip Mo used to sit on my front porch, and I braided his hair while JJ and Jamie C. from Oak Street Posse pulled up in their

5.0s; they claimed Blood. It was beef, but over the wrong things, which led to Crip Mo's baby's momma getting killed in front of the sheriff's department and a child getting killed on Oak Street.

The end of my ninth-grade year was slowly approaching. We had our prom, and I invited Ryan McElroy. He didn't go to our school, and he was considered a pretty boy. Pops escorted me, Tonya, Ryan, and Bernard to the prom in his Lincoln. We wore red, and it was the first time I wore makeup. My mom took me, Kim B., and Kiji to Dillard's to get the makeover. After the prom, we went to the bowling alley, and afterward, Pops dropped everybody off. From time to time, he would steal him a feel on my vagina and reminded me it was his and that I better not be giving it to nobody. Little did he know he had turned me into freak.

I was turning fifteen, and since I couldn't play ball, I would make me some money. I got a job at Showbiz Pizza for the summer of 1990. I worked in the game room, the kitchen, and I would dress up in the suit for birthday parties. I saved my money and bought me lots of tennis shoes.

High School

LITTLE ROCK CENTRAL High 1990 was the year to be there. I had so much fun at Central my sophomore year I didn't want the year to end. I didn't play volleyball because I wanted my knee to be 100 percent for basketball. I went to all the football games, and I still messed around with Rick. He finally made it official: I was his only girl. We took pictures together, and he was still the apple of my eye.

I was picked to walk on the football homecoming court. I asked my brother Kaelon to walk me; we wore dark blue. I was so excited that night until some boy touched my booty, and Kaelon and Rick beat him up real bad. We left the field, and I went over Rick's for a little while, and then we went to the state fair.

The fair was a big thing in Little Rock. Everybody went to the fair. I managed to get away from Rick for a little while, and I began to get more into the streets. I met Wallace Sims. He was a big-time dealer in Little Rock. Wallace had been shot and left for dead in a ditch by his so-called friend. When I met him, he was paralyzed from the neck down. I used to suction him out when he got full of phlegm. Nikki, Mut, and Tina took real good care of Wallace after he became paralyzed.

Wallace would come pick me up from school in his white Transport van. It had so much sound in it you could hear him coming two blocks away. I felt sorry for him because he had two beautiful children that he never had an opportunity to hold. Me, Nikki, Wallace, and whoever was his driver that month went everywhere. We loved going to the movies on Asher and Professor Bowl. Everywhere we went, he kept his pillow on his lap, and his pistol under it. Wallace had much respect in the streets, and being with him gave me more respect in the streets as well.

Wallace knew I was young, and a lot of dope dealers had been trying to get at me. He told me to be honest with him and never disrespect him. I was always honest with him, and I never disrespected him; he was the one I went to for advice, and he told me which guys not to deal with.

After Wallace, I started dating Sed; he was my oldest brother's classmate. I was about to turn sixteen, and the high school boys were not catching my eye. Sed worked, and he had some major connections in the street. I wanted to be in the hood, hanging with the thugs, and I couldn't see that it would be no fun in the end.

Sed had a California connect named Dee. He was Belizean mixed with black. Tall, slim, and very handsome. A month into our relationship, I met Dee. We were at Sed's apartment, and Sed went into the back to get Dee's money, and Dee stood up and rubbed against my booty. Two weeks later, he called me. He got my number from Jan, my nail tech.

Dee showed me another side of hustling. He would come in town for a week and would be gone the rest of the month. He would come get me at 2:00 a.m., when my mom went on her paper route. I would stuff pillows in my bed, go out the back door, run down the alley, and jump in his white Cadillac. We would go to the Super 8 Motel, off Scott Hamilton and lie up until five; I had to beat my mom home. We never got caught, and he always had me back on time. I told him I was sixteen, but I was really fifteen. I was turning sixteen in a couple of months, so I lied just a little.

Our principal, Mr. Hickman, let us have lip sync. I performed Mary J. Blige. The lip sync was fun, and it gave us something to look forward to next year. I maintained a 3.5 GPA because I had dreams of going to Spelman College in Atlanta. My cousin Dee Dee told me about the school, and after looking into it, I wanted to go.

School was going good, basketball was coming along, but I was so lost. I went everywhere, I did everything, and I still didn't have any direction. My tenth-grade year was coming to an end, and my friend, who was a senior at the time, wrote me a letter; and it let me know that I had let the streets take over me.

The letter read:

Kenya   4/18/91

Well . . . It's about that time that we a sister talk/friend talk about you & life in general. I've noticed (others too) that you've changed and not for the better. The people you hang around have reputations that are somehow rubbing off on you. I'm just saying that you should take a look at yourself and see if you can see the change. The companies (boyfriends) you keep (as of late) have all been dealers; that's not the problem though. You seem to be taking on their lifestyle, and that's not you. I know you might hate me for saying this, but I'm telling you this because I love ya dearly. And if you ever need to talk about anything I'm just a telephone call away. I was hurt when someone told me about you calling them talking about something that Demont was thinking about doing . . . It's not worth it & think of all the people you would be hurting like me. If ever you want to talk to someone about your dad I'm here. Take it light.

Luv ya like a sis
Toi!
Ya partner in crime

I knew then that I had become uncontrollable. The senior prom was in two weeks, and Merlan Devine asked me to go to the prom with him. My brother Kaelon took Latise Mays, and I went with Merlan. We wore black, and after the prom, he took me down to the River Front Park and played the saxophone for me. It was so romantic. I should have hooked up with someone like him, but instead, I chose thugs and lowlifes.

The summer of 1991 I worked at Little Rock Neighborhoods and Planning. It was a job through the state for teens. Dee came back and bought a three-storey house in Sherwood. He had a Corvette and a Jeep Wagon. I stayed at the house a lot when he went to California, but I got lonely when he was gone, and I continued to see other guys.

Zay was an older cat from Highland Court projects. He was a big-time dealer, and after he found out I dated Rick, he didn't feel bad talking to me. He lived in Out in the Woods apartments off Kanis, and my friend, Janana's sister, lived there too. I would always spend the night over Janana's so I could go see Zay.

I remember one night, I wanted to go spend the night over Janana's, and I think my mom realized what I was doing, and she told me no. I went crazy. She pinned me down on the ground, and I thought I wanted to rise up against my mom, but I was wrong.

My eleventh-grade year was about to start. I was still messing with Dee and Zay, and I started feeling nauseous, so my mom made me a doctor's appointment to see Dr. Hearne. His office was located off Twelfth Street. My mother couldn't take me, so I had to take myself. An hour later, I found out I was pregnant. I called Dee and told him, and he told me to get an abortion. My doctor gave me the number to an abortion clinic and suggested I get it done.

Dee sent his partner down there from LA to take me to get it done. Deron took me to a clinic off Markham, and after the procedure, we went back to the house in Sherwood. While I was lying there, Dee's woman called. She asked who I was, and I told her. I asked her who she was, and she told me. After that, I didn't hear from him for a month. I couldn't sleep for weeks, and I got into a deep depression. I never told a soul about what I had done, and I felt so bad for doing it, especially after he treated me the way he did.

Manny started going to Central, and he bought me lunch every day, telling me he wanted me to be his woman. I was picked to be on the football homecoming court again. I asked Manny to escort me, and we wore orange. After the homecoming game, I spent the night with him at his apartment. He was sixteen, and he already had his own place. He fixed me dinner that night after homecoming; we had greens and pork chops and corn. It was so romantic.

Manny was like none of the other guys I was with. He loved me, and he showed me. I just wasn't ready to be with one person. I didn't know how to love because I never felt any, and I had been through so much. I really didn't trust any men. He wrote me a letter that read this way:

Konsuela, [that was the nickname he gave me]

Hey babe. What's up with you? How are you feeling? Is your chest still hurting? Well if it is, you know who to call, me right? Baby I'm going to get right down to business. Ok. I would like to start off by saying dido" or "shub-be-do-be-bo whop." Also Sunday was a very exciting day for me also. Because I didn't think you were going to go with me. I was just going to see what you were going to say. But, it turned out ok. I still wish I could have made love to you. Hey but it's just one of them things. But, we should spend more time like that together, and I wish you would consider spending alot more time with me. Even without me asking you. You should want to spend time with me, more. But anyway thanks for the apology but I don't want apologies anymore. I want you to stop doing the things that you do, or the things that hurt me especially. Baby I'm not being mean on these next few lines so don't take it like that. I'm just telling you the way I feel. Baby, it's as simple as this. I want to be with you and nobody else. And it's not my decision if we get back together or not. Its yours because you hold the key. But, it doesn't seem like you want to use the key nor do you? Shell it's like Tracie Spencer said "I'm so confused" and you are so unpredictable. Well that's how I feel and you can change that feeling, if not I want us to be friends, but that's not what I really want. But that's what you are making me decide. Cause see I've given you a lot of chances. And I know that you may feel like hey I'm not going to keep waiting on him either you going to go back with me or you going to leave me alone. But that's not fair for the things you have done and I'm still here for you when you need me. And I also know that you can make it without me too. But all that's really beside the point. Shell you say you love me and you want to be with me and that you apologize for what you done. And that you love your man, me. And that what I tell you then that's what you will do. But Shell I've heard this from you before and what did you do? And you seem to be more sincere each time. And I want to believe you but it's hard because I'm afraid that you'll do it all over again, and then I might kick your ass (smile). See I need real examples and proof that you mean what you say. Actions speak louder than words. Show me Shell that you really mean it. Show me please. See you don't know how I feel when people like Ray ask me about our relationship. Because he knows some things and it makes me feel just like Stacy, and I be damn if I keep being treated this way because I don't deserve it. And I don't give a damn about what nobody says. But it is deep when I feel the same way about myself. So Shell if you truly want me and I mean the world to you, then goddamn it show it, and tell it and mean it. Don't play with me either. Shell I want you to show me, How deep is your love and about you having "kicking it friends" the fuck or hell with that. How are you going to have friends, male friends to kick it with, especially when they like you? A couple girls cool, but niggers, hell no. And not alot of girls either. Cause they cause trouble. And I know everything you do doesn't have to involve me, I want you to have freedom, but to keep me in mind when you're out. Plus how do you think that looks, you go with me but you go out with Tre, ride with Derek, and etc. I don't see how you can do it. And it looks bad on both of us. Cause I'm supposed to be your man. People probably think I'm some kind of fucking punk. But this must stop; you must start respecting me if not yourself. But I'm going to get you right if you going to be with me. Also I guess that when I told you that "3" couldn't come over while we were together as soon as I said we aren't together anymore oh he's over every day I still think that if you cared anything about me you would still respect me. Shell how do you think I felt tonight when I got over and he was there? I said to myself I'm glad I didn't bring any cheese sticks, because I would have felt like a damn fool. He probably would have felt the same about me. And how much stress do you think it puts on me when your family (who I like and like me) sees me and another individual over to see you. I feel especially bad around your mom (my mom). She told this lady at the store that I was hers too. I was touched. But that makes it even worse. You know? See you need not to see those people at your house anymore. But regardless I'll still be there, cause aint no other guy going to run me off. Like tonight I wasn't leaving until he left. But I have nothing against him (I like the cool cat) and you said in your letter that if that's the way I want it then, you have no choice but to accept it. And that's what I want. Just me and you and there should be no pressure right? So Shell baby just show me if that's what you want for us to be together. Cause that's what I really and truly want. And Baby, darling I truly adore you and that's what I'm listening to. Baby you are my heart and mind. I truly told you that I'll be there for you, and I mean it. Baby if I haven't gotten the surprise you told me about last night then I'm looking forward to it. And I have a surprise for you Friday night and day. And speaking of Friday I can't wait it's going to be Fiii, but baby its 12:53 and I'm sleepy so I love you and I'll see ya.

Mansuelo

Ps. There's a "right and a wrong way to love somebody" and a good and bad way also. So take your time and choose the one you really want to do.

He was in the tenth grade, and I was junior at Central High. He had grown women trying to get with him because he had a lot of money. He had a lot of female friends, and I had a lot of male friends. He only wanted me to be with him, but I couldn't. I don't know if I was scared or if a part of me just had to have more than one man in my life. I attributed it to not having my father in my life, no guidance or support from anyone.

Manny and I went everywhere together. He loved taking me out of town to go shopping. We went to Memphis almost every weekend. On the drive back, I would always jack him off; that drove him crazy. He was making major money, and he had major connections, so money was no issue with him. I was the only issue because I couldn't be faithful. Dee kept coming back in town with his sad story, and I always fell for it.

One night, Manny was at my house, and Dee pulled up. He knew Manny was making money by the cars he drove, and he did not want to lose me to this younger cat. I also met another guy from LA named Trey. He hung around Crip Mo, but he was a Blood from Compton. Trey had some other guys he was dealing with, Al and Fink. I happened to run into all the dealers from California. I never sold drugs because I didn't have to, but I hung around everyone that did.

I didn't go to the clubs because I was too young, but I stayed in the streets and around the dealers. Manny couldn't take any more after the night Dee came over there, and he told me if he couldn't have me to himself, then he didn't want me. This crushed me because I really did care about him, but I knew I wasn't ready to be with just him. He had several women he was seeing; he just didn't want me to mess around with any other guys.

Basketball season started; Coach Fitzpatrick was our coach. He taught me a lot, and he always told us, "Pressure bust a pipe." My friend JS and I had gotten close after junior high. I spent the night over her house a lot. Her mom was respected in the corporate world, and they were very well off. We played basketball, and her mom took us to Shreveport to see our friend, Derek, play basketball. They played Memphis State, and after the game, we went to Derek's dorm, and I took everybody's money, shooting craps. We had so much fun in school. We used to dress alike and wear our hair alike, and I hooked her up with some of the street guys I was messing around with. One weekend, we went to Memphis with her mother to go shopping, and Ledell and Clint met us up there. Ledell tried to holler, but he just wasn't my type. He was making money, but not enough for me.

JS's mom went out of town, and she stayed with her dad for the weekend. We decided to go to Jacksonville skating rink one Sunday night. Her dad told us to be in before her mom's plane landed. We were having so much fun; the time flew by. When we realized how late it had become, we hauled tail to get back to Little Rock before her mom made it home. I was driving my brother's SS Impala, which Dee had sold him. They went to New Orleans, and I was only supposed to pick his car up and park it. I wanted to show off at the skating rink, so I drove it. I was going 75 mph on 67 South, trying to get JS home. The car cut off past the McCain Mall exit. I pulled under the overpass, and the car started smoking. We lifted the hood, and smoke and fire went everywhere. JS had a water gun in the backseat, and she got it out, trying to put the fire out. I couldn't believe it; my brother was going to kill me. We ran to the pay phone to call my mom and her dad. The fire department came and put the fire out, and our parents took us home.

My brother got in late that night, and I heard him ask my mom where his car was. She told him it burned up. He didn't talk to me for three months. They went to New Orleans to see my brother's friend, Al, and he gave me specific instructions to pick his car up and park it; I just refused to follow directions.

Little Rock had become gang infested and drug infested, and I was a part of them both. Nineteen ninety-one brought about a lot of senseless killings. I watched my classmate get killed at Wheels and Grills. Me, Wallace, and Nikki were in the first stall closest to Martin Luther King Street. Wheels and Grills was packed – the parking lot was full, all of the stalls were full, and people were driving through at standstill traffic. Rob, Bernard, JJ, and a couple of the other guys from Oak Street had rode through in Nate's car, and they left. Nate came back to the carwash in his car. They entered on the Wright Avenue side of the car wash. Traffic was at a standstill when I noticed a guy get out off the back of a pickup truck with a sawed-off shotgun. He pumped and fired. It hit the front window, and I saw two guys jump out the car and run east, out of the parking lot, as the guy continued shooting. Everybody at the car wash got down, and they started speeding out the parking lot. I had to go see who was in the car, and if they were alive. I told Nikki I would be right back. When I got to the passenger side of the car, Nate blew a bubble of blood out his mouth, and I knew he was dead. He was shot in the forehead and in the side, and Bernard was shot in the butt, but he lived.

I started getting close to JJ from Oak; he would come by my house and sit out and talk with me for hours. He had a friend, Ced (Cake Mix), who liked my friend Janana, but she was getting ready to move to Louisiana with her mom. We would all go to the movies and then go to the motel on University. JJ was getting money, but he kept a lot of guys around him. They called themselves the Oak Street Posse (OSP), and we called ourselves LPB (Lady Pimpin' Bloods). Manny didn't like the fact that I was getting close to JJ, so he always wanted to come get me and wine and dine me.

Manny got himself a girlfriend named Trina to make me jealous. She didn't go to Central, but all of her friends did. They hated me because Manny loved me. They hated to see me talk to him, and they made sure he saw them when we were together. We were both in other relationships, but we still got together whenever one called the other.

I tore my ACL again playing basketball, so I walked on a cane, and I had to have another surgery. My eleventh-grade year was going good until the rumors started. They said my mom got up in Trumpet and Zion and asked the church to pray for her because her daughter was HIV positive. My relatives started calling from California to Detroit. Is it true? Does Shell have AIDS? I thought I was going to have to kill somebody. I knew I wasn't HIV positive, and I was going to get to the bottom of who was spreading this rumor. I knew Manny's girlfriend's friends were behind this, so I kept asking and finally got a name of who was spreading this lie – Jenn, a girl whom I had beef with since junior high. She had a bunch of sisters, and she thought she was tough.

One night, JS and I went back out to Jacksonville Skating Rink, and when I walked in the door, everybody started coming up to me, telling me Jenn was in there. I walked around to find her because I was gonna crack her dead in her mouth. I worked at the prosecuting attorney's office for the summer, so I knew how to get out of any trouble. When I saw her, I walked up to her and asked her why she was spreading lies on me. As soon as she opened her mouth, I hit her; she swung back, and next thing I knew, JS came across the rail and hit her in the eye. Security rushed to the fight, and they kicked us out. On my way out, a guy named David Tidwell tried to holler at me; I told him I would meet up with him later.

Jenn's older sister came to my job, trying to prosecute me; she said I hit her sister with a skate, but that was a lie. It didn't hold up, and I wasn't prosecuted because I was seventeen, a minor. The summer was coming to an end, and I had been to LA with Dee for a couple of days. I was still kicking it with JJ, and Manny wanted to take me to Dallas to go school shopping.

Manny, Dexter, Sporty, and I jumped in his extended cab gold truck and headed to Dallas. He was into it with Trina because she wouldn't come get his money and take it home. He said, "Forget it. Let's just go." We got to Sulpher Springs, Texas, and the police got behind us. Manny and I were in the backseat asleep; Dexter and Sporty were in the front. The police came to the window and asked Dexter to step out of the truck. Dexter got out with no shoes on, and Manny told me to put four stacks of hundreds in my purse, and he wrapped the rest in his coat.

The police came back to the truck and asked us for our identification. I handed him mine; Neither Manny nor Sporty had an ID. The officer asked us to step out the truck. I had my purse on my shoulder, and we left the coat in the backseat. When we got in the police car, the first thing they brought out was the coat of money. Me, Manny, and Sporty were in one car, and Dexter was in the other car. They took us to the police station, separated us, and questioned us.

I told them we were going to Dallas to go shopping and that I worked at the prosecuting attorney's office; they told me I didn't know who I was riding with, and they were going to buy drugs. I knew that was a lie. They searched me and my purse and took the money out my purse because it was wrapped in rubber bands, like the other money they found. They pulled out a video recorder and made us sit in the room with them as they counted the money on tape. It was $30,000. Manny was sick. They let us go, but they kept Dexter because he warranted in Arkansas.

We had no money, but I did have my brother's credit card. We went to the Holiday Inn and got a room. He called Trina and cursed her out. He told her to be out his house when he got back. The next day, we posted bail for Dexter and waited for him to be released. We didn't make it to Dallas; we went back home.

JJ's best friend, Ced, got killed that summer. Janana came home and thought we were going to kick it with them again, but a crackhead killed Ced on Oak Street. I went to the funeral with Manny, and I wanted to be with JJ so bad, but I knew he would be okay.

My senior year was finally here. Mr. John Hickman was our principal. He put you in the mind of Joe Clark from the movie *Lean on Me*. JJ started going to Central. Manny went to Central, and, boy, did I have my hands full. JJ didn't make it long. He was too far into the streets. Plus, he was getting ready to be a father in a couple of months, so he dropped out.

We had another lip sync, and this year, Smitty and I did Mary J. Blige and JoJo's "If loving you is all that I have to do." We rocked the show. Mr. Hickman let me emcee the lip sync, so during intermission, I played "Rumors" by Club Nouveau. I told the audience this song was for all the haters who said I had AIDS. After the lip sync, Trina and her friends waited to jump on me. My brothers and cousins were all there, and they made me get in the car, and they beat up all the girls who were trying to jump me.

I was picked to be on the homecoming court again. I could have won queen, but a lot of girls were telling people not to vote for me. Manny escorted me again; he bought me a beautiful black-and-gold dress, and we walked proudly together. After the homecoming, we took Matt home; he lived in Village Square, and he walked Lamonia Perry on the homecoming court. Matt and I became best friends after that. He was a two-year senior, and he was popular at the school. We went to the state fair that night, me, Stacey, Manny, and Zay. I hooked Stacey up with Zay, and me and Manny got a room. After homecoming, Manny and I began to drift apart, and even though I wasn't kicking it with JJ, we still got together sometimes.

One night, I went to the bowling alley with Manny, and Trina came in with her friends. Manny told Dexter to take me to the car. She went to the pool table with JJ like she was in there with him, and Manny beat her up pretty bad. All her friends blamed me, but I didn't have anything to do with it. She tried to make him jealous 'cause he was with me, and she knew I used to kick it with JJ so that was a butt whooping she created.

I met Ray at the bowling alley in Southwest, Little Rock. He was a Belizean from California and was down there making money. He was connected, and he had plenty of money. He was dating a girl that lived in Village Green named Angel. He asked me to come over and spend the night with him at her apartment. We talked all night until we fell asleep. He had an off-white Range Rover that he drove and a gray Chrysler as his underbucket.

He came in town like Dee used to do. I went to school half the day, and I worked the other half. Ray wanted me to go to Las Vegas with him, so me and Janana went. She was down for whatever; we lied about where we were going, and we never got caught. We drove the truck – me, Ray, Janana, and Ray's cousin Denz. We went to Las Vegas to drop off some money. We stayed at the Mirage. He was a Platinum Plus member. As soon as we walked in the door, he gambled $20,000 on the crap tables. I was seventeen years old, and money had become the root of all evil for me.

We flew back to Little Rock, and Janana told everybody where we had been. This made Manny very upset. He called me and told me he needed to talk to me. I told him to come get me. Me, him, Dexter, and Sporty went to their room at the Days Inn off Sixty-fifth Street. They had adjoining rooms, and Manny and I went to one side, and he closed and locked the door. He started going through my purse. I think he was high or had been snorting cocaine because he was not acting himself. He started lighting matches and throwing them at me. I asked him to take me home. He saw the pictures we took in Vegas in my purse and he snapped. He threw me on the bed and forced his penis in my vagina. I begged him to stop, but he continued until he came in me. This was the second time he didn't use a condom.

New Year's Eve 1992, Tasha and I went to a party on W. Twentieth. JJ came and he wanted me to leave with him, but I had promised Ray we would spend New Year's together. After the party, I had Tasha drop me off at the Holiday Inn Express by the airport. Ray was pissy drunk. He told me three months was long enough for him to wait and if I was going to give him some. We had sex, and he fell asleep.

My mother was about to move from the house on Thirteenth, and I refused to go. I wanted to stay in the hood, so I slept on the couch for about a month. Ray bought a house in Southwest, and I stayed with him most nights when he was in town. Valentine's Day 1993, Ray bought me a bulletproof vest because he said I had so many enemies, and he gave me some money to get me some lingerie. He bought a Jacuzzi for the house, and that was our place to make love.

Ray was short, very light skinned, and he had long hair. He had a few homeboys in town, and they all looked out for me. Ray loved for me to be with him. We drove to California several times, and his family was very nice to me. He had two sons and a daughter, and every time we went to California, the kids would come to the hotel with us, and we were a happy family.

I took Sonya with me to California on a trip. Ray drove the Range Rover, and Sonya, Jay, and I went along for the ride. We had the boat attached, and the wind was so high the boat started swinging. Ray was such a good driver. He held it under control because the truck almost flipped over. He had the Jet Ski on the boat, and I think it was too much weight for the Range Rover. Sonya and I stayed for a couple of days; we went shopping, and Ray flew us back to Little Rock.

The females in Little Rock began hating me because I was driving a Range Rover in twelfth grade. I kept my hair done every week, and

I always wore clothes nobody else had. They began telling Ray I was still messing with Manny and JJ, and he believed them. I actually was faithful to Ray until he started messing with Felicia. When I found out, I called her boyfriend, Mark, and he beat her down real good.

I always gave the guys I dated the benefit of the doubt. I gave them one chance to mess around on me, and after that, I would go into my dog mode. I hated to be lied to, and I hated to be lied on. I started picking up weight, and Ray asked me if I was pregnant. I told him no. March 1993, I was getting ready for the prom, graduation, senior banquet, and I missed my period.

I told Ray, and he asked me if I wanted to get an abortion. I told him to let me think about it. My mom had a water bed that sat high up off the floor, and I got in it and rolled onto the floor. My eighteenth birthday was here, and I was going to have a baby. I didn't know how to tell anybody, so I kept it to myself.

Wallace and I still communicated, and one day, he brought David Tidwell to my house to meet me. He was from the north side. He drove a Cadillac, and he and his daddy were getting paid. They had a club in Jacksonville that we hung out at often. We would shoot pool and listen to Whitney Houston's *The Bodyguard* CD. I loved going to Club Cameo because everyone there was older, and I made a lot of connections there. David asked me to spend the night with him, and my homegirl Charlotte was with me, so he hooked her up with his homeboy. We went to the Holiday Inn in North Little Rock. I had a hair appointment the next morning, and as he was dropping me off, Ray pulled up in front of us and blocked David's Cadillac. He got his gun and asked me who he was. I told him that he was my man. He told me to call him and let him know I was all right. I got out his car and walked up to the Range Rover. Ray was looking pissed. He asked me where I'd been. I lied and told him David gave me a ride to the beauty shop. He told me to stop lying and that he'd followed us since the night before. Charlotte had called him and told him where we were because she was dating his friend Buck. I didn't care; he was messing around with Felicia, and even though I was pregnant, I wasn't going to be dogged out by no man. I had applied to Spelman College and was waiting to find out if I had gotten accepted. That was going to determine if I got an abortion or not. There was a bad flood in the southern region of the United States, and that delayed the mail for two weeks. I knew I was getting further along in my pregnancy, and it was going to be too late to get an abortion if I kept waiting. Finally, I got my letter from Spelman. I didn't get accepted. That was my answer; I was going to keep the baby.

Ray got indicted on drug charges; they raided the house and took my bulletproof vest along with a lot of money. I'm glad I wasn't there. April came so fast; my senior year was almost over. Manny asked me to ride with him to Indianapolis to visit Dokes. I rode with him because I wanted to tell him I was pregnant.

We hadn't had sex since he raped me at the Days Inn, and it was a chance that he could be the father of my child. When I told him, he was excited. He told me that if the test proved he wasn't, he didn't want me to tell anybody, and he was still going to take care of it. I felt bad because I didn't know who the father of my child was. When we got back to Little Rock, JJ's baby's momma told Manny she was pregnant by him too.

I went to my senior banquet with Michael, a white boy from my school. We looked marvelous. No one could believe I brought a white date to our banquet, but I didn't care, I always had to be different. Shanolda and I sung at the banquet, and I won best dressed, most popular, and best hair. After the banquet, we went to Miles Reed's house for a party. I stayed for a little while, and I left Mike to go be with JJ.

I told JJ I was pregnant, and he asked me if it was his. I told him I didn't know, but I thought it was Ray's. He said he wished it was his, and he would help me with whatever I needed since Ray was locked up.

My senior prom was magnificent. I took Rick and JJ. We wore off-white. My brother's girlfriend, Sherri, helped me get ready because my mom was out of town. I thought Sherri would notice the weight I had gained, but she didn't say anything. I met JJ at his mom's house in River Ridge to take pictures. I told him I would meet him at the prom. I left and went to pick Rick up. We had a great time, and after the prom, I dropped Rick off at his mom's house, and I went to Club Cameo. I was finally old enough to go to the club, so I started clubbing, pregnant and all.

I threw a party for the seniors at Pennick Boys and Girls Club. I hired a DJ, charged to get in, and sold pizza. The party was jumping;

everybody from all the high schools came. After the party, my mom dropped me off on Thirteenth, and as I was getting out the car, she asked me if I was pregnant. I told her yes. She asked me if it was by David. I said no, that it was by Ray. The next day, she made me a doctor's appointment to see Dr. Chang. I had to take all kinds of tests, and they gave me an ultrasound. It was a boy. I went to see Ray, and I showed him the ultrasound pictures. He was excited; I was five months pregnant and didn't know what the future held for me and my baby.

After High School

J UNE 1993, I was a proud
graduate of Little Rock Central
High. David came to my graduation and brought me a dozen roses
and a diamond ring. I spoke at our graduation, and even though our
principal had gotten fired for sexual misconduct, he instilled a lot of
discipline in our class. He bought my baby bed for me, and I had a
lot of respect for him. It was because of him that me and a lot of my
classmates graduated from high school. I went to Project Graduation
at Slick Willies with Matt. We took pictures all night, and afterward,
we went to Club Cameo. Matt couldn't have been a better friend to
me during this time.

After graduation, I went to summer school at Hampton University
in Hampton, Virginia. I wanted to attend an all-black college, and
since I didn't get accepted to Spelman, I applied to Hampton and
got accepted. I planned to attend summer school to get ahead on my
classes, go back home, and have the baby; and after I had the baby, I
would move back to Virginia to finish school.

While at Hampton, I met a lot of friendly people. Nobody knew
I was pregnant, and I didn't tell anyone. A football player for the
university started liking me. He would come to my dorm with gifts
for me, but I really didn't want to get involved with anyone because I
already had a lot going on. Another student named Keith Taylor from
Mississippi showed interest in me. He was real sweet, and he allowed

me to open up to him and tell him everything that was going on with me. Keith and I spent a lot of time together on campus, and he was my best friend at Hampton for the summer.

My brother Kaelon had a girlfriend that attended Hampton, so he drove up to see us. We went to the movies, and it was my first time off campus since I moved up there. We spent the night over Latise's house, went to the movies, and they took me back to school on Sunday, and they went back to Little Rock. I talked to Manny, JJ, and Matt every day while I was at school. I had so many phone calls; it caused me and my roommate to fall out. She was from New Jersey, and she had friends from home that attended summer school with us. She began to get on my nerves so bad that one weekend she went home. I moved her stuff to her friend's room and asked her friend's roommate to transfer to my room. Her name was Camille, and she was from Newport News, Virginia, thirty minutes from the college. She was much friendly, and she was never in the room. We stayed on the tenth floor of the dorm, and Keith would sneak up to our room to stay with me some nights. We didn't have coed dorms, so I would sneak in his dorm on the weekends and spend the night with him.

Dee called me and asked me to fly to Houston to see him. I had Camille to drop me off at the airport, and off to Houston I went. He was still upset with me for getting pregnant, but he didn't want me to keep his child. He took me shopping and bought me a lot of maternity clothes, and he wined and dined me for the weekend. I hated to go back to school, but I had to finish the summer classes. When I got back, Keith and I had a long talk about our lives. I realized I still didn't have a clue about life. I was looking for love in all the wrong places. I didn't have a relationship with anyone in my family to express my feelings, so I kept them bottled up inside.

I finished summer school with a 3.5 GPA, and I couldn't wait to get back to Little Rock. Manny picked me up from the airport, and he told me he was going to come see me. But somebody told him JJ was coming, so he changed his mind. He asked me if there was a chance that JJ could be the father; I told him no. So he made me promise him that if he was not the father, I wouldn't tell anyone, and I would let my child grow up thinking he was.

He asked me to fly to California with him to get away. I did, and we had a good time. His uncle was living there, and he showed us LA.

We went shopping, played pool, and hung out everywhere. Manny was still dating Trina and April, but he was still in love with me. When we got back from LA, he started his senior year at Central, and I was getting ready to give birth. I had two months left, and I decided to give myself a baby shower at Murray Lock and Dam. I invited all my friends from school and my family. I got a lot of nice gifts, and I was ready for my baby to be born.

October 3, 1993, Manny got a room at the hotel behind Breckenridge Movie Theatre. He had never had sex with me that rough before. It felt like he was trying to make this baby come out of me. After we got done, we walked to the movies. I began to feel sharp pains, so I went to the bathroom because it felt like I had to use it. I wiped myself and saw a pinkish color on the tissue. I told Manny to take me home; I lived around the corner from the movies, so he dropped me off.

When I got there, I told my mom I was hurting. It felt like I had to have a bowel movement. I was sitting on the toilet, and as I was pushing, I saw the top of my baby's head. As I was on the toilet, Ray called. I told him I was having contractions, and he told me good luck, and he was going to call me later to see if I had the baby. My mom told me to stop pushing and get my bags; she was taking me to the hospital. We arrived at St. Vincent's at 10:30 p.m. The nurse prepped me, and they gave me an epidural. Manny's grandmother peeped her head in to let me know she was there. I had only dilated four centimeters, and I had to be at ten before I could deliver the baby. The doctor got to the hospital after I dilated seven centimeters, and they told me it shouldn't be much longer. Mrs. Albright, Manny's grandmother, came in and told me she was going to be there until I delivered the baby. My mom was there with me, and I began to get anxious.

At 2:03 a.m., October 4, 1993, my baby boy was finally here. He was so handsome. I didn't know what to name him, so I decided I would wait a day before I named him. They took him to the nursery because his blood sugar was low. I had so many visitors the next day; I guess everyone wanted to see who he looked like. I didn't care as long as he had all his fingers and toes and was healthy, I was happy. Manny came by, and he went to the nursery to hold him. He said he looked just like him. I couldn't see it. I thought he looked like me, but I wasn't in the mood to argue. The doctors released me, but they kept the baby an extra day to get his blood sugar leveled. Manny took me back up to the hospital the next day to pick him up. I named him Kyron LaJuan Richardson.

I breast-fed him, and I promised him that he would never want for nothing. My baby was healthy, seven pounds, six ounces, and had a head full of hair. Ray wanted to see him; I told him he would have to wait six weeks before we could travel. His friend gave me the money to fly to Springfield, Missouri, to see him. It was so cold, but we had a good visit. He played with him, and he said he looked like his oldest son when he was a baby.

I had two baby daddies and three men wanting to be. Matt had a friend named Tega who started liking me. Tega was from Granite Mountain, and he was making major money in the streets. He bought Kyron every pair of Jordans that came out, and there was nothing he wouldn't do for me. I was still playing games with JJ, Manny, Dee, and whoever else would let me.

I went to Club Cameo every Thursday, Friday, and Saturday. I provided for my son, but I didn't give him any motherly affection because I didn't know how. All I wanted to do was get my hair done every week, buy me a new outfit, and keep my son dressed in the latest fashion. I took several trips, running dope in and out of Little Rock.

I hooked up with Bop from Dixie in North Little Rock. He ran a gambling house, and he was pushing major dope through Arkansas. He had several women, so I didn't get my feelings too involved in him. He bought me anything I wanted, and he kept my hair done.

Manny and I were still communicating, but April, JJ's baby's momma, had her baby a week after I did; and because I wasn't with him, he didn't do as much for me as he did for her. Our sons looked like they could have been twins, and that made Manny feel like Kyron was his. I didn't ask anyone to do anything for my child because I was making money, and I wanted to do it all so no one can say I had them taking care of a child that wasn't theirs.

JJ asked me to move to Houston with him because he felt like he was going to get indicted. I took Kyron and his son, Li'l Jay, and we drove eight hours to our new home. We stayed with his friend Lawrence and his family until Jay found out what was going to happen to him. I got home sick and wanted to come back home. I moved back before Christmas 1993, and I wished I could've stayed.

Dee was still coming in and out of town, and we still hooking up whenever he was in town. He loved Kyron like he was his own. He flew us to California and Las Vegas every month. He had his women in both states, but he managed to keep me happy. We drove to St. Louis to pick up some work because the guy couldn't move all of it. We drove back to Little Rock, and when he dropped me off at home, a Federal agent named Mark Stafford had left a business card on my mother's door with my name on the back to contact him as soon as possible. I called my dad and told him about it. He told me he was going to take me to meet the guy.

I didn't know if we had been followed from St. Louis, or if I had been caught doing something else. My dad and I went to the office, and my dad knew the FBI agent. He told me I wasn't in any kind of trouble; he just needed to ask me a few questions. I sat there, looking puzzled, and he asked me about Ray. I told him that I had been involved with him before he got locked up. Then he started asking me about JJ. I told him I had been involved with him as well. He asked me if had I been around any drug activity with either of them. I told him no. He asked me if I knew JJ sold drugs. I told him no. He asked me how I thought he got all those fancy cars and house. I told him I thought his mom had money. He was getting upset with me because I wasn't cooperating. He told me that if he had any other questions, he would contact me. We left the office, and my dad told me to be careful because they were going to be watching me.

My nineteenth birthday was coming up, and my son was getting bigger. I didn't know what I wanted to do with my life, and I still running the streets and going to the club. I went to visit Ray, but we began to grow farther and farther apart. David was still around; Nikki and him had a baby, so we would talk on the phone and go out to eat, but my mind was on making me some money.

Bernard got killed in a motorcycle accident on Twelfth Street. All of Oak Street Posse was getting killed or locked up. JJ fought his case for a year, but they found him guilty of conspiring to sell cocaine and of being the leader of a gang. I went to Bernard's funeral, and at the funeral, Derrick Gunn, who was working for Will Acklin Funeral Home, told me that I should move to Dallas and go to Pierce Mortuary College. He gave me the phone number to call and I called. I had to get away from Little Rock before I got indicted or killed.

I carried two pistols on me at all times, and I continued to hang around the gangbangers and thugs. I smoked weed every day because I couldn't handle all the drama in my life. Manny graduated from Central, and he told me he wanted to move to California and wanted me to go with him. I flew up there with him, Dexter, and Head. His uncle and his uncle's girlfriend, Pam, picked us up from the airport. We stayed in Hollywood at the Manchester Hotel. Manny had big dreams, and even though both of our boys were in Little Rock, he was planning for their future.

We went shopping every day and got high all day. My third day of being out there, Manny had spent over $10,000 on clothes. He bought him and his uncle tuxedos, alligator vests, Versace glasses. We went shopping on Rodeo Drive and ate at all the fancy restaurants. One morning, he told me to ride with his uncle's girlfriend, and he would catch up with us later. She rolled up twenty joints, and they took fifteen with them and gave us five. We rode around LA until they called us. Manny's uncle told us to meet them at the mall. When we got to the mall, Manny was walking outside in his boxers with no shirt on. I asked Dexter what was wrong with him; he said he had wigged out.

We got back to the hotel, and his uncle told us to get ready. He wanted to take us out to a club. He had a brand-new purple Lincoln Continental with gold Dayton and Vogue rims. We pulled up to the club, and his uncle got out at the front door. Me, Manny, and Pam drove into an alley to turn around. Manny started telling me to change clothes in the car. He wanted me to put on a jumpsuit. I told him to stop tripping and he snapped. He got out the car while it was still running and told Pam to go park it. When Pam got out, some gangbangers ran and jumped in the car and took off. We had just gotten carjacked. We went in the club, and I told his uncle what had happened. He couldn't believe it; Manny was still going off on me because I put on the wrong jumpsuit. The men at the club thought I was stripping, and they told me I could change in the bathroom. Pam called the police, and Manny's uncle was mad because we were in a bad neighborhood and could possibly get killed for calling the police. We had to sneak out the club and get a ride back to the hotel. When we got to the hotel, Manny started tripping so hard. I called his grandmother in Little Rock and told her he was acting strange. I felt like someone had slipped him a mickey or had laced his weed with something. She told me to call her back if he didn't act any better when he woke up. We went to bed, and at 4:00 a.m., the hotel security knocked on the door. He said someone needed to come downstairs and get Manny; he was sitting outside, butt naked, on the curb. I went next door to his uncle's room and told him what was going on. He went downstairs and got Manny. When Manny came back in the room, he started licking me all over my body, and then when he got done, he went in the bathroom and started playing in the toilet. I told his uncle I was scared and I wanted to go back to Little Rock. I went across the hall to Dexter and Head's room and asked them what had happened to Manny. Dexter said when they came and picked him up from some girl's house, Manny had started tripping. The next morning, I called his grandmother and told her she needed to come out there because he was losing his mind, and I would stay until she got there.

She flew out there the next day, she and Li'l Manny. Manny was still not himself; he was talking crazy and acting crazy. His uncle bought me a ticket home, and I left. Three days later, they called me and asked me to pick them up from the airport. When I got there, undercover police were everywhere. His uncle thought I had called them, but my mother's phone was tapped. When we got their luggage and went outside, the police walked up to us and asked if they could check their bags. They let them, and they even asked to check the baby's bag. I took them to Manny's house on Gaines Street. When we got there, Manny's uncle started tripping. He told me to tell Manny to stop tripping and tell him where his money was. I realized that what had happened in LA had something to do with his uncle. I left and went home. And the next day, I found out Manny had been held hostage in his house, and the police had come and took Manny to jail.

I applied to Dallas Institute of Funeral Service and got accepted. I went to Dallas in July 1994 to find myself an apartment. My mom and my friend Yolanda drove down and found a nice apartment that was not too far from the school. The weekend we went down, I met Kenneth Long and Maurice Robinson. They were from Dallas, and they told me to call them when I moved down there, and they would show me around. I started class August 1994, and my life made a turn for the better, until . . .

Dallas, Texas

I MOVED TO 1615 John W. Boulevard, Dallas, Texas. I didn't have a car, and I left my son in Little Rock with my mom. When I got to Dallas Institute of Funeral Service, I met several people from school, and I caught a ride with my classmates to and from school. Byron Baker and his older brother, Daniel, attended the college with me, and they showed me around Dallas. Byron lived with his mom in Oak Cliff, and we got close until I met Jeff. Jeff was an older guy who lived in Dallas all his life, and he wasn't trying to sleep with me; he took me in like a little sister. He schooled me on pool, and he introduced me to Dallas. Jeff's wife owned a beauty shop on Buckner, and that's where I got my hair done. Tracie Lawson was the best hairstylist in Dallas, and she used to hook me up. Tracie and I became good friends, and she took me out a lot and introduced me to a lot of people in Dallas. Jeff and I used to hang out at Sparkles Detail Shop off Lancaster, and the owner, Theron, used to try to hit on me. Jeff wouldn't allow me to mingle with any of the men there; he wanted me to meet "Mr. Right." We shot pool at Speeds on Camp Wisdom every Friday and Saturday nights. That's where I met Pat E. Pat had just got out the Feds, and he had major money. His grandmother stayed in Oak Cliff off Saner, and that's where I spent a lot of my time when I wasn't at school. School was interesting and very difficult in some areas. I learned a lot about embalming, and I said if I could finish, this would be the field for me.

I got a job at UPS, and I worked the five-to-nine shifts. I was blessed with a job in the high volume/loss prevention department. I keyed in items worth $500 or more that came in our *hub*, or items that was lost or stolen. I enjoyed working, but I enjoyed spending time with Pat more. He let me use one of his cars to get to school and work. One night, he came over, and he was high off sherm, and we were in my living room when we heard a noise outside. It was Byron; he was creeping around my apartment to see who I was messing around with. I stopped talking to him because he stopped going to school. Pat was more mature, and I found out that he and Byron had a run-in before over another female. Pat was mad because I didn't tell him about Byron, but it wasn't anything serious. We went to school together, and he gave me a ride home when I needed it. Pat left and I went to Little Rock for the weekend.

My son was turning one, and I decided to throw him and Li'l Manny a birthday party at Chuck E. Cheese's in North Little Rock. Manny was locked up, and he couldn't make it. Everybody else came, and after the party, I said I would never do it again; I would have my son's party for him only. I went back to Dallas, and the following week, Dee and Kyron flew down to see me. We were still close, and even though he had things going on, he kept in touch with me. We had a good time, and I hated to see them leave.

I had a friend named Tina, who was trying to get her singing career off the ground. She moved to Dallas with her mother, but her mother said she was getting out of control. I didn't see myself as a positive role model, but I could show her how to play men and get money. We met some Jamaicans, and they spent money on us. We clubbed every weekend and met people from everywhere. I loved going to Big T Bazaar. I met African Jimmy there; he owned a clothing store, and his cousin was trying to talk to me. He stole a lot of clothes and money from Jimmy, and no one could find him. Jimmy called me, and I told him I hadn't seen or heard from him. Jimmy came over to my apartment and started trying to have sex with me. I wouldn't take my pants off, and he ground so hard that he came all over my Girbaud jeans. He was so embarrassed that he got up and left. I tripped out. I told Jeff about it, and he fell out laughing. He told me that's why he didn't want me messing around with anybody from Dallas unless he knew them.

I went walking a lot by my apartments. I met Tre one day while I was walking. He drove an extended cab truck like Manny had. He was driving east on John West, and I was walking back to my apartment. He made a U-turn and came back to talk to me. We exchanged numbers and went from there. He was from South Dallas, and I could tell he was getting money. He came and got me over the weekend, and we went to shoot pool. He was cool, and he knew a lot of people that I had already met. We talked and he told me he had a woman, so I didn't get my feelings too tied up in him.

I was missing Pat, and I started calling him so we could hook up. My homeboys from Arkansas came down to buy some pounds of weed. I hooked them up, and I got a cut of the profits. I rode back to Little Rock with them, and we had the weed in the trunk. We stopped in Hope, Arkansas, to break open a bag so we could smoke on the road. We smoked all the way home, and we got to town in time to go to the club. I still loved going out when I got home, but I tried to spend as much time with my son as I could because I was missing him.

I flew back to Dallas, and I took my son with me. When he got there, I had to find someone to watch him while I went to school, but Pat looked out for me. We took him everywhere, even to Speed's to shoot pool. Pat didn't have any kids, so he was excited to have a little boy with him. After the holidays, I took him back to my mom and started looking for day cares because I wanted him to move to Texas with me until my second drive-by.

Pat and I went to shoot pool every weekend. One night we didn't go to our usual spot, Speed's; we went to a pool hall off Kiest. He was waiting on some people to come down and get some work. They met us at the pool hall, and while we were shooting pool, Pat's cousin, T, went outside to use the pay phone. Ten minutes later, he ran inside the pool hall out of breath, telling Pat someone had pulled a pistol on him. We jumped in Pat's car and went looking for the Mexicans. As we approached a light, T recognized their car. Pat told T to get the gun out of the secret compartment and hand it to him. T gave Pat the gun, and as we got up on the car, Pat pointed the gun at the car, but the gun didn't go off. I handed him my derringer as the car sped off, and Pat started shooting at them. The car hit a few corners, and we lost them. We went back to Pat's grandmother's house so they could get some more guns, and Pat told me to go home.

My homeboy Bernard had just gotten out the pen in Little Rock, and I asked him to move to Texas with me. He came and he got connected with all my people when he got there. Bernard and Manny were locked up together, and he wrote Manny and asked him if he wanted him to move with me. Manny told him yes. Manny had a silver custom-made suburban that was parked at his house in Arkansas. He also had an old-school blue Delta 88 convertible that was in Irving, Texas, with his cousin Sharee's boyfriend, Mack. He wanted me to get the old school out the shop because he had gotten the hydraulics taken off. He also told me to get the suburban and take it back to Texas with me. Manny's father, Bruce, was locked up in Wrightsville unit, and he had me to visit him when I came back in town.

Bernard and I drove it back, and I got so much attention from driving that truck. Me and Bernard went to meet Tre one day, and he thought I had hit a lick when he saw the truck. He took me and Bernard to the shooting range every time he got a new gun. It gave me a rush every time I pulled the trigger, and I became a pretty good shooter. Tre was cool, and even though he had a woman, he still showed interest in me.

Dee called me and asked me to make a run for him, and I told him I would. He gave me my flight information, and I had Jeff drop me off at DFW airport. I forgot I had the .357 derringer that Jeff gave me in my makeup bag. I was about to miss my flight, and I had to take my luggage on as carry-on. I sent my bag through the security, and an old man, about eighty years old, was there at security checkpoint. He sent my bag through, and he kept seeing an object, but when he opened up the bag, he didn't see the Derringer. He opened my makeup bag and took out my black-and-gold Donna Karan perfume bottle and said that must be what he kept seeing. I said yes and that I was about to miss my plane. He zipped my bag up and told me to have a good flight. I was so nervous, but God made it possible for me to get on that plane.

I got to St. Louis, and Dee picked me up from the airport. We drove an hour away, and he begged me to sit on his lap so he could get some. It was snowing, and we were driving having sex on the freeway. When we finally got to the hotel, he explained to me what he wanted me to do. He took me shopping to buy me a business suit. He said I needed to look professional and to take off my jewelry. He said Joe was going to pick me up from LAX Airport and not to touch the bag, to let the skycap get the luggage. When I got to LAX, as I was going to baggage claim, I noticed a lot of undercover police looking around. I didn't get nervous; I did exactly what he told me to do. I went and sat on a bench outside, and I had the skycap guy to sit the bag next to me on the curve. Joe was late, but I'm glad he was because they were probably looking for his car. A Los Angeles undercover officer sat next to me, flashed his badge, and told me I wasn't in any kind of trouble. He was just doing routine questioning. He asked me where I was coming from. I told him Dallas. He asked me what I was doing in Los Angeles. I told him I was coming to take care of my sick aunt. He asked me what I did in Dallas. I told him I was in Mortuary College. He was impressed. He began to ask me how to embalm, and I began to explain it to him. He told me that was interesting, and he told me to be careful and have a good trip. When he walked away, I grabbed the luggage and went and caught a cab to the Hilton Hotel, down the street from the airport.

I called Joe and told him where I was. He came and got the luggage and took me out. We went to a club in Hollywood. I met Shaquille O'Neal, Zeus "Tiny" Lister, and all kind of celebrities. After the club closed, we went to a restaurant where a lot of celebrities hung out. Joe, Lester, and I sat down to eat. And Zeus came over, and I took pictures with him, and we exchanged numbers. I had a great time in Los Angeles, and I hated to leave. Lester was Dee's cousin, and he took me back to the hotel. He came up to my room, and of course, he tried to have sex. I told him no, but he forced himself on me. I begged him to stop, and after he came, he did. The next morning, he took me to the airport, and I flew back to Dallas.

I told Bernard how good of a time I had, and he asked me if I wanted to go back. We drove Manny's suburban out there, and we stayed with Joe. We went everywhere. I had other friends that lived there, Fink, Face, and Damion. I took Bernard over to Fink's house, and he had a dirt bike that Bernard begged to ride. They asked me if he knew how to ride. I told them I didn't know. Bernard got down the block and fell. They ran to tell me my homeboy had hurt himself. I told him that's his fault, and I told him if he didn't know how to ride, he should not to get on. I made him drive himself to the hospital because I couldn't believe he had gotten on something he didn't know how to ride. The next morning, Fink took me back over Joe's house. Dee had called and found out I was in LA. He was pissed off. He started telling me to leave and not to go back to Joe's house. He was really mad because he found out about me and Lester. Bernard broke his leg, and I was mad because I was going to have to drive all the way back to Dallas without his help. Joe gave us a pound of weed to smoke, and we left, going back to Dallas.

We got to Bakersfield, California, and the police pulled us over. They pulled us over because the windows were tinted too dark. The police came to my window and asked me for my driver's license. I handed him the insurance papers and my driver's license. He came back to the truck and asked me if he could search the vehicle. I asked him why. He asked me if we had any drugs in the vehicle. I told him I had a sack of weed, and I gave it to him. He went back to the police car and told us to get out the vehicle. They put us in the police car and searched the vehicle. The pound of weed was in my suitcase. They took me to the station and told Bernard he could drive the vehicle to pick me up once I got fingerprinted. I had been caught with my first charge. It was a misdemeanor, but it was going on my record.

I made Bernard help me drive because I was tired. We finally made it back to Dallas, and Pat called. We were supposed to meet at Speed's at nine, but he didn't show up. While we were there, Bernard gambled my cell phone away. I was pissed. A short guy came out to the truck and told me he could get the phone back if I gave him my number. As we were talking, Pat pulled up. He asked me where I was going, and I told him I was going home. All the guys in the pool hall were looking outside to see what I was going to do. The guy told me his name was Anthony. I gave him my number, and he went in and got my phone back. He followed me home and asked me to go out to eat with him. I dropped Bernard off, and I followed him to Denny's. We ate, talked, and went back to his house.

Wedding Bells

ANTHONY WAS FROM Dallas, lived there all his life. His parents owned two beauty shops, and his father owned a tax service. He was impressed when I told him what I was doing in Dallas. He told me he had a baby on the way, and the girl had just broken up with him. He had just bought her a blue Mercedes, and they were living in Oak Cliff. The night we met, he showed so much interest he would not let me get away from him. I came to Little Rock for the weekend, and he came with me. He met my family, and I took him to Club Cameo. He was such a gentleman, and he gave me anything I wanted. He knew I loved to shoot pool, and to keep me from going out, he bought me a pool table. He asked me to move in with him, so I let Bernard keep my apartment. A month later, I found out I was pregnant. He said he wanted to marry me because he didn't want to have children scattered all over the United States. I told him he would have to ask my daddy, so he called him. My dad told him he couldn't give him that kind of permission over the phone. My twentieth birthday was coming up, and Anthony told me he wanted to get married on my birthday, and I agreed. I called Matt and told him, so he flew down to Dallas and witnessed my wedding. We went to the Justice of the Peace, and Matt brought me a turkey sandwich from Uncle T's and a cake from community bakery that was my wedding gift.

I was so happy, and I couldn't believe I had actually gotten married. His parents were not happy because they were on a cruise at the time, and no one knew or approved of us getting married. We were young and thought we were in love. His baby was due April, and the baby's momma did hair at his mother's salon. She had a boyfriend, so she didn't care that we had gotten married. Manny was upset because I had his vehicles, and I had gotten married without telling him.

I was still attending school, and Anthony wanted me to move Kyron to Dallas with us, so I did. April 28, 1995, Courtney was born. He went to the hospital to be witness of the birth of his firstborn. He was a very good father to Kyron, and I knew he would be a good father to Courtney and to the child I was carrying. We bought a detail shop on the corner of Ledbetter and Houston School Road. Excalibur Detail Shop was the name of it. Every baller in Dallas came and got their car washed there. On Sundays, the park was jumping, and we charged people to park on the parking lot of the detail shop. We made a lot of money, and Anthony was a born hustler.

One day we were at the detail shop, and Kenneth Long pulled up. He came in and spoke to me. I didn't know he had Pat in the car with him. When I saw Pat get out, I didn't know what to do or say. I hate that I didn't tell Pat. I just stopped calling him. I left the detail shop, got in the Mustang, and drove off so fast. I didn't realize I still had the emergency brake down. I just had to get away from there. Anthony knew I was crazy about Pat, but he didn't say anything to me. He just let me leave. When I got back, they were gone, and Anthony didn't say a word about it.

The summer was approaching fast, and I had two months of school left. My father-in-law purchased us a ticket for a cruise that he was taking the whole family on. Anthony, his mom, his three sisters, his father, and me went on a seven-day cruise on the Royal Caribbean cruise ship. I had a blast. I was five months pregnant and big as a house, but I still enjoyed myself. We went to St. Thomas and the surrounding islands, stopped to go shopping and toured the different islands. We took so many pictures on and off the ship, and we treated it as our honeymoon. When we got back, I didn't know what happened, but Anthony wanted to move to Arkansas. I told him that when I graduated we could move. August 1995, I graduated from Dallas Institute of

Funeral Service. My mom, Matt, and brother came to my graduation. I was so happy to be out of school. I just didn't want to move back to Little Rock because I knew why I had left, and I didn't want Anthony to get caught up in the hype. But of course he did.

Word to the Wise

ON'T LOOK AT other people and assume they got it going on because you never know the struggles or the sacrifices that were made to get what they have. You should never judge a person if you don't know what they have been through, and even if you think you know, only God can judge them.

Parents, it's important that you pay attention to who your children hang around with. You can't know your child's every move when they get a certain age, but you can establish a relationship with them so they will feel comfortable enough in sharing their deepest secrets with you. Mothers, we have to teach our daughters that they don't have to wear skintight clothes to get attention from boys because they could be attracting men and sexual predators while wearing provocative clothing.

Young women, you don't have to settle for any man or boy nor do you have to have sex to prove your love for them. It's okay to save yourself for marriage. Sex is a bond that God created for husband and wife. Don't try to trap a man by getting pregnant because in the end, you will be raising a child alone. Don't let a man try to trap you by getting you pregnant. If you save yourself for marriage, abortion will not be a thought in your mind. It's time we start living for God and doing what pleases him. After all, we were created in his image; and for him to bring us through the trials and tribulations that we create for ourselves, we can give him enough respect to do his will. If you don't know him, get to know him. With all I went through in this segment of my life, I couldn't have made it without him.

The journey on the next ten years of my life, you will see that there has to be a God for me to be able to stand and testify about his goodness. May God bless each of you, and I hope my testimony is able to help someone realize that just because your innocence may have been stripped from you, you can still make it. God has a purpose for each of us, and it's up to us to find out what that purpose is.